IZZY BIZZY
GOES TO THE ZOO

Created & Written by **PENNEY JACK**   Illustrated by **CRAIG REX PERRY**

Bizzyworks LLC.

Chicago, Illinois

IZZY BIZZY GOES TO THE ZOO

Published by

Bizzyworks LLC.

Chicago, Illinois

Email: SUNSUM1234@AOL.COM

Penney Jack, Publisher & Editorial Director
Kim Norton, Editor
Craig Rex Perry, Illustrator
Yvonne Rose/QualityPress.info, Book Packager

ALL RIGHTS RESERVED

No part of this book may be reproduced or transmitted in any form or by any means electronic or mechanical, including photocopying, recording or by any information storage and retrieval system without written permission from the author, except for the inclusion of brief quotations in a review.

You may contact the Publisher at SUNSUM1234@AOL.COM

Copyright © 2018

ISBN # 978-1-7323308-0-1

Library of Congress Control Number: 2018906825

One day Mama and Papa Bizzy took Izzy Bizzy or Bizzy Izzy as they called her to the zoo. The zoo was Izzy Bizzy's favorite place to go.

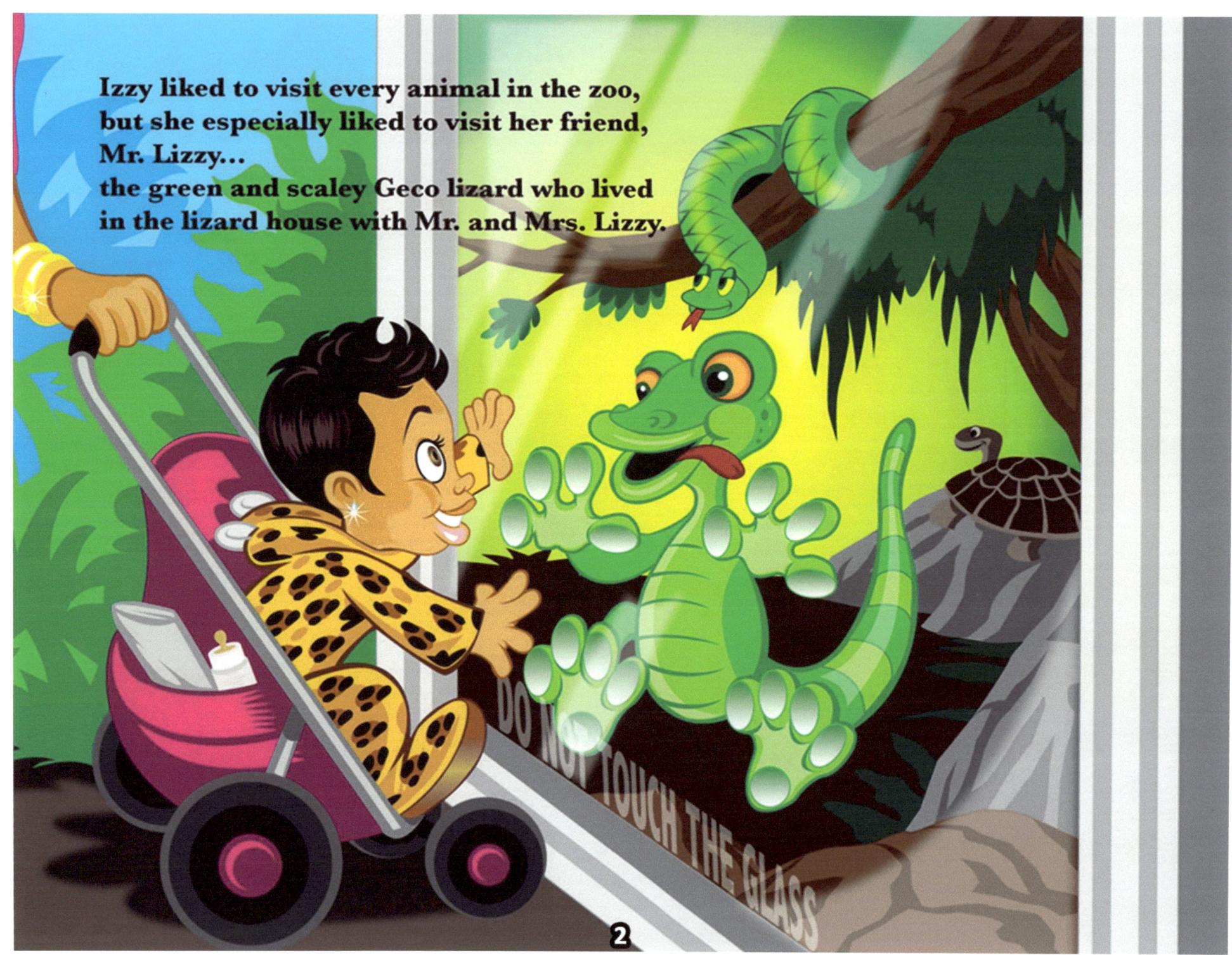

Izzy liked to visit every animal in the zoo, but she especially liked to visit her friend, Mr. Lizzy...
the green and scaley Geco lizard who lived in the lizard house with Mr. and Mrs. Lizzy.

Izzy always felt sorry for Mr. Lizzy, because he looked so sad as he watched the Bizzy's, as free as his friends, the Birdie Wirdies, flying gleefully through the air making whirlie twirlies.

He looked especially sad when the Bizzy's would have to say good-bye. Izzy would always tell Mama Bizzy that Lizzy was in a mizzy! (Izzy meant miserable!)

Daddy Bizzy would try to cheer Izzy up by saying, "Izzy Bizzy, don't worry, Mr. Lizzy will keep bizzy with Mama and Papa Lizzy until we return."

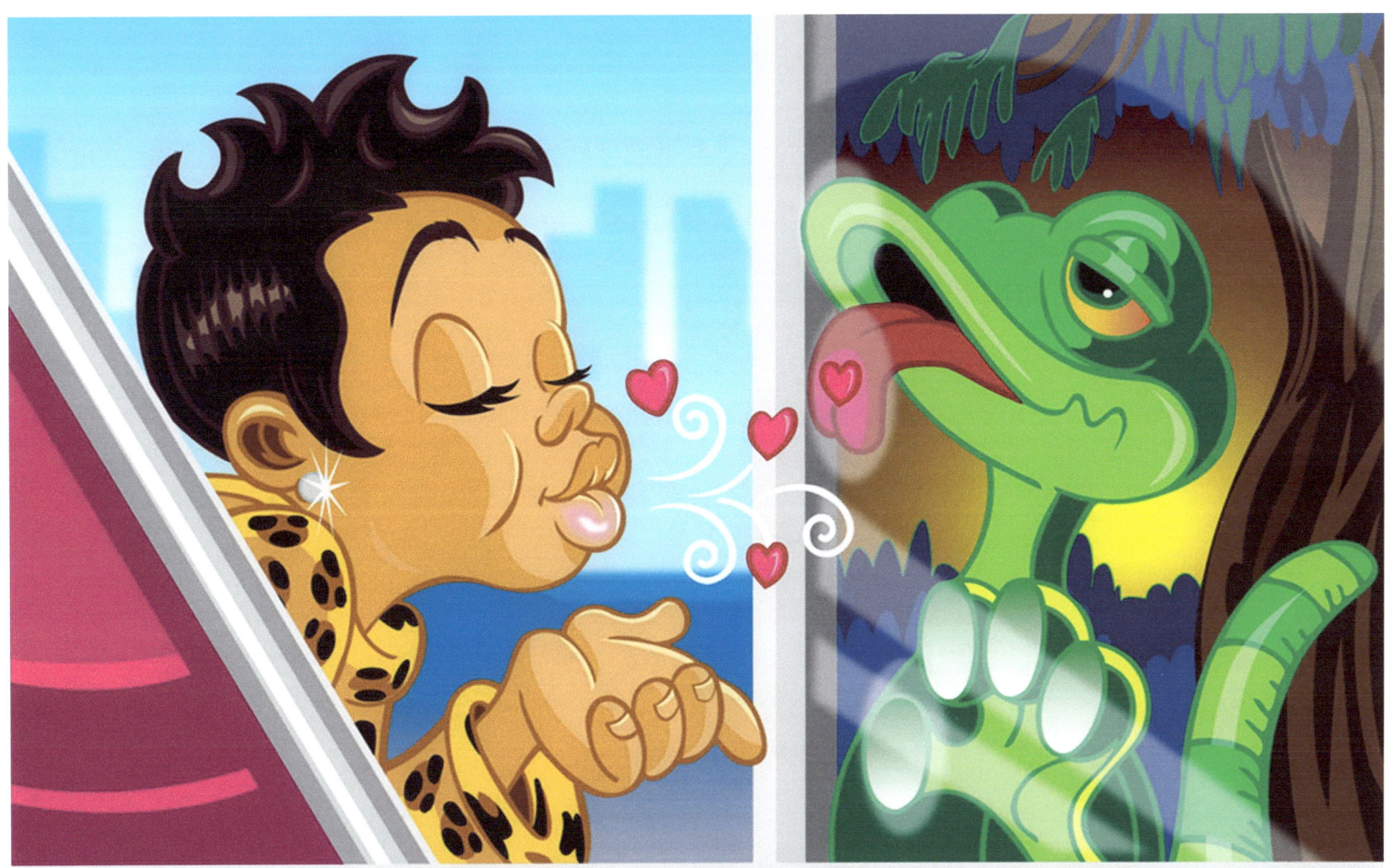

This never made Izzy Bizzy feel better, so she blew Mr. Lizzy a kizzy, (Izzy meant a "kiss"), through the shiney-whiney glass window that separated Izzy Bizzy and Mr. Lizzy.

This day however would be different.
Izzy Bizzy or Bizzy Izzy as the Bizzy's called her,
vowed not to leave Mr. Izzy behind!

On this day, the keeper of the lizard house accidentally left the big, shiney-whiney door of the Izzy's house open while he went to get more food. Izzy Bizzy saw her chance!

Izzy Bizzy reached into the Lizzy house and put Mr. Lizzy in the special gray colored Lizzy sack Mrs. Bizzy had knit for Izzy.

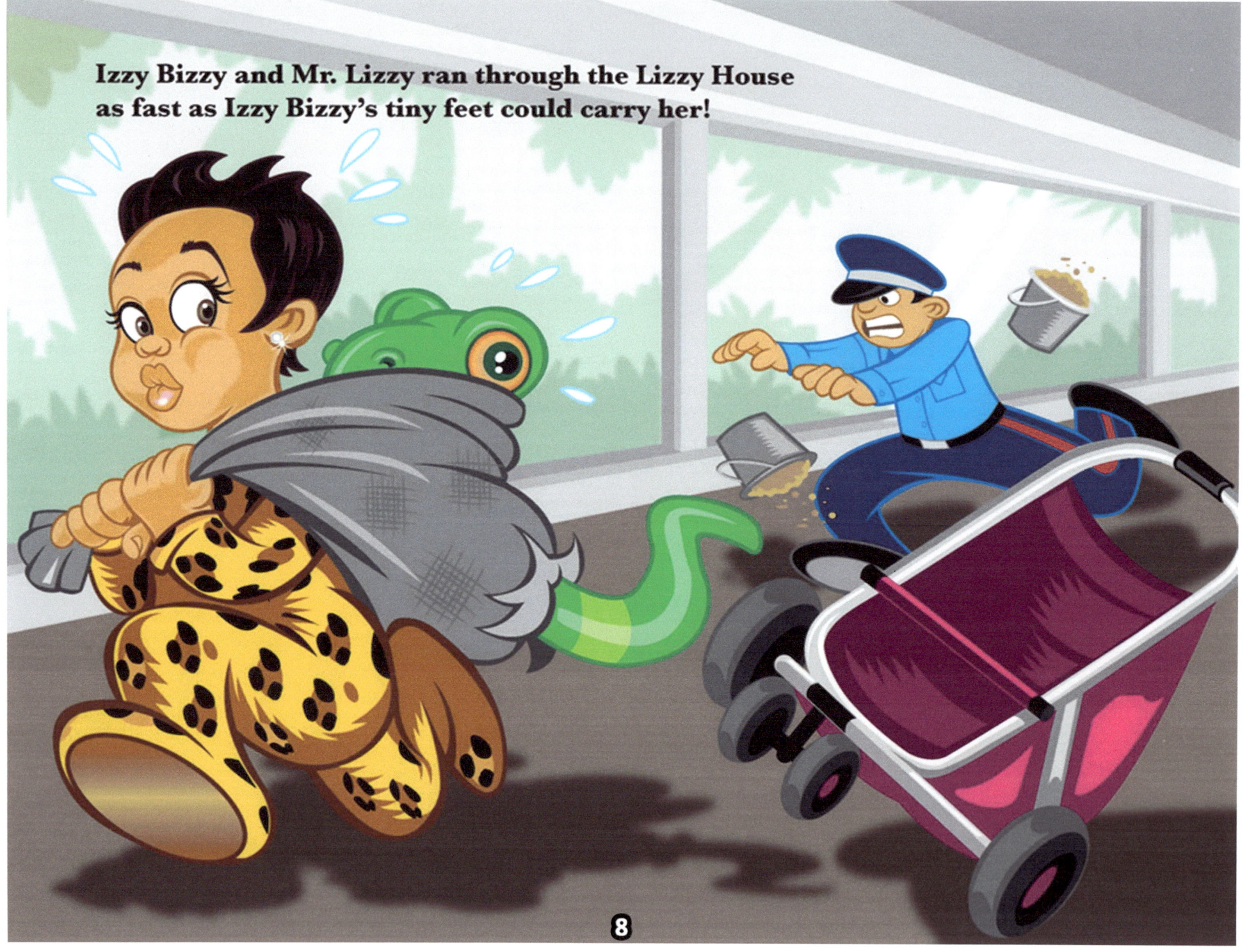

Izzy Bizzy was in a tizzy as Mr. and Mrs. Bizzy ran after her calling "Izzy Bizzy or Bizzy Izzy, you'd better get back here right now. You're scaring Mr. Lizzy!"

Izzy Bizzy and Mr. Lizzy ran so fast through the lizard house, all the other lizards saw this as their chance to escape!

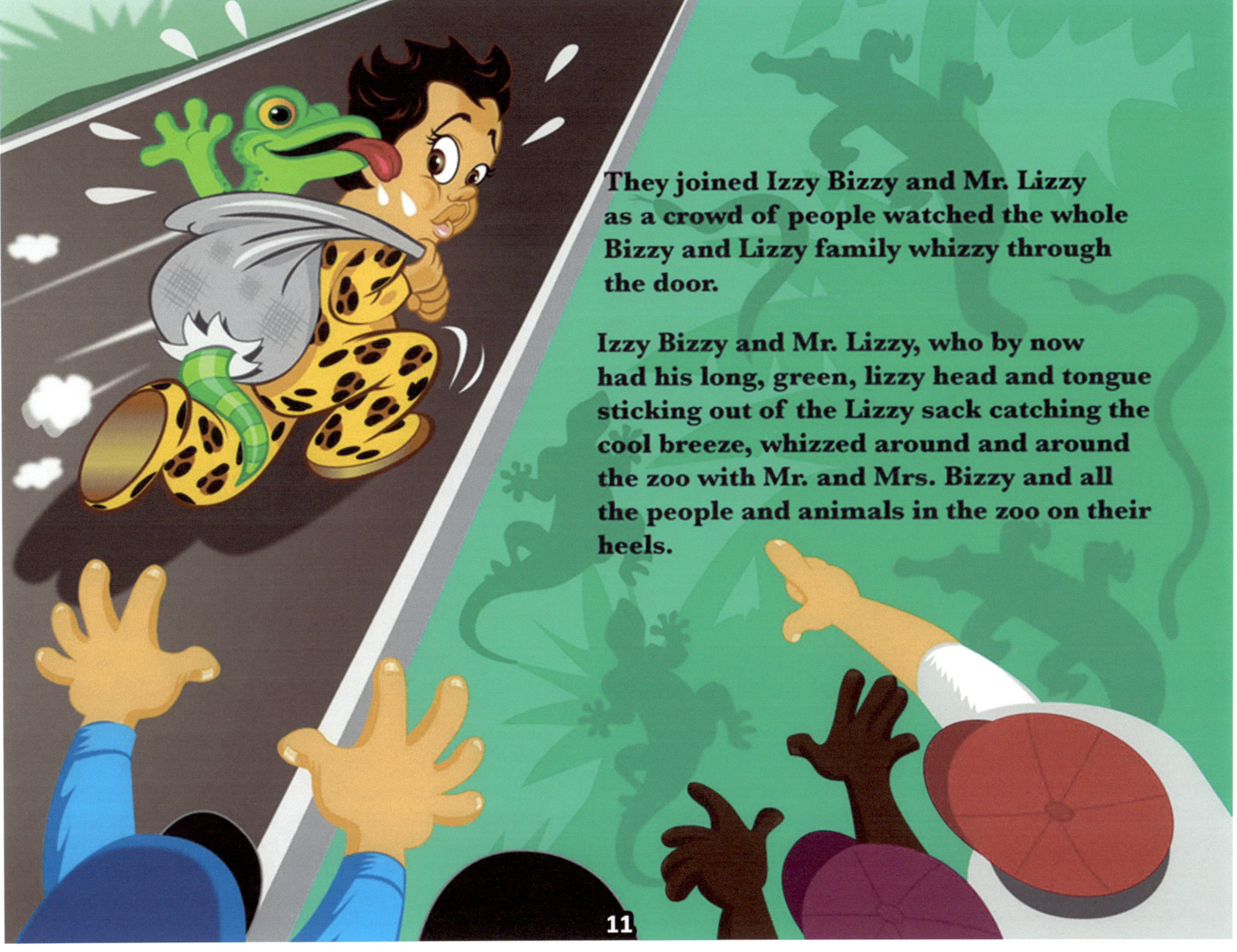

They joined Izzy Bizzy and Mr. Lizzy as a crowd of people watched the whole Bizzy and Lizzy family whizzy through the door.

Izzy Bizzy and Mr. Lizzy, who by now had his long, green, lizzy head and tongue sticking out of the Lizzy sack catching the cool breeze, whizzed around and around the zoo with Mr. and Mrs. Bizzy and all the people and animals in the zoo on their heels.

She had caused such an uproar,
Izzy Bizzy thought it best to make her way back to Mr. Lizzy's house
and there she waited until Mr. and Mrs. Lizzy crawled in behind him.

By now the Bizzy's and everybody else in the zoo had returned to watch Izzy Bizzy blow Mr. Lizzy a kizzy goodby as she had always done.

Before she left, she thought it best to explain to Mr. Lizzy that she felt sorry for him because he was locked up behind the shiney-whiney, glass window house he called home.

Now, she explained to Mr. Lizzy, she knew indeed he was as happy in his home with Mama and Papa Lizzy...

Everybody in the lizard house, including all the animals said, "Ahhhh!" And gave Izzy Bizzy a round of applause.

Izzy Bizzy blew Mr. Lizzy a kizzy as she has always done...

...and Mr. and Mrs. Bizzy took Izzy Bizzy or Bizzy Izzy, as the Bizzy's called her, and left for home.

I wonder what Izzy Bizzy's next adventure will be? Don't you?

DEDICATION

I dedicate this book and those to follow
to the start of this journey.

To Rodney Jack Sr.,
my husband, whose wings and spirit
watch over me every day.
and
Craig Rex Perry,
the illustrator, who is drawing
IzzyBizzys and PaigeyWaigeys
in the sky.

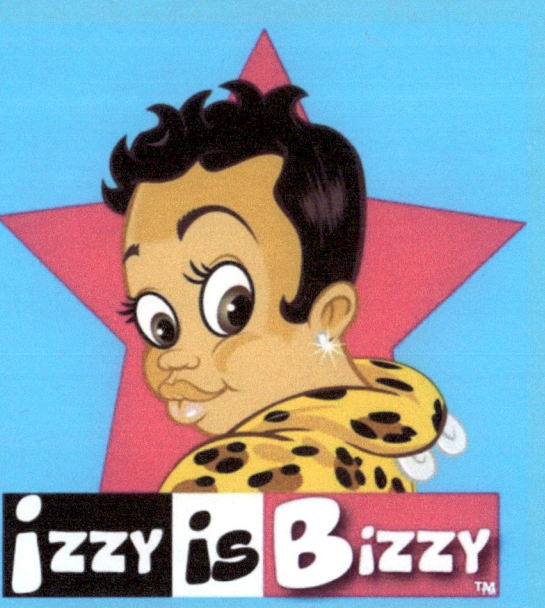

ABOUT THE AUTHOR

Penney Jack is the author of the 'Izzy is Bizzy' children's book series. Penney Jack is a retired school teacher and educator with a passion for children's literature. Her love of children is the inspiration behind this heart-warming, classic series. "I love being the child, the parent, the grandparent and anyone else that smiles when they read a story they too can
Imagine."

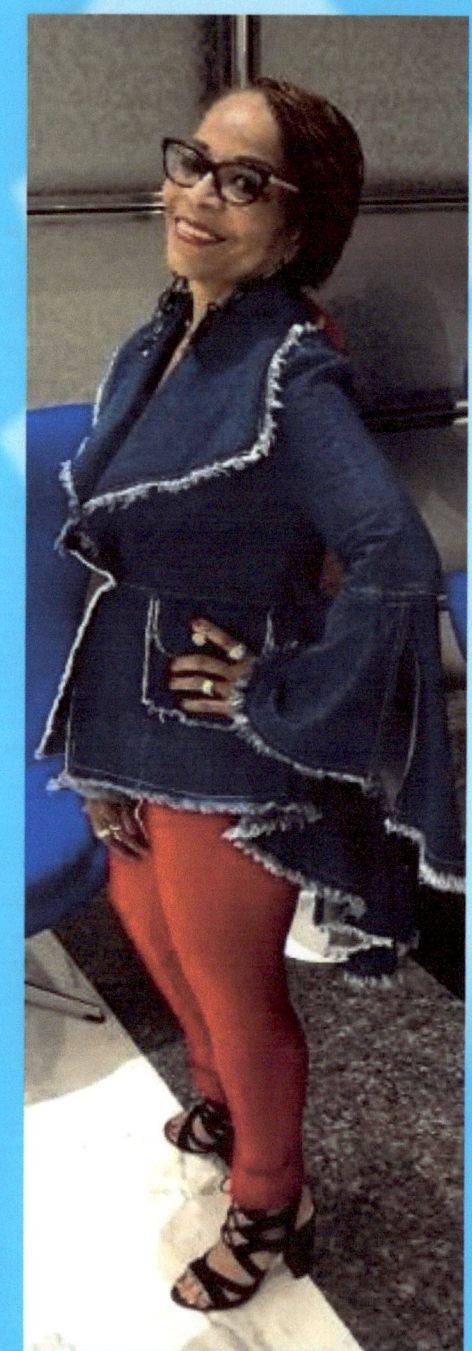

www.ingramcontent.com/pod-product-compliance
Lightning Source LLC
Chambersburg PA
CBHW041155070526
44584CB00004B/312